FOR ALL TIME

Me and my galaxy: Stargazer
Jack Suman of Tucson, Ariz.,
combined a photo of himself with
an early morning shot he took of
the Milky Way to create a star-
studded composite.

FOR ALL TIME

A PICTORIAL CELEBRATION OF AMERICA
BY THE WINNERS OF THE PARADE MILLENNIUM PHOTO CONTEST

INTRODUCTION BY LEE KRAVITZ

WITH REFLECTIONS BY
EDDIE ADAMS, YOGI BERRA, DR. JOYCE BROTHERS, ENRICO COLANTONI

2000

The Continuum International Publishing Group Inc
370 Lexington Avenue, New York, NY 10017

The Continuum International Publishing Group Ltd
Wellington House, 125 Strand, London WC2R 0BB

Design by Robin Bernstein and Adam Kline

Printed in Hong Kong

Library of Congress Cataloging-in-Publication Data
For all time : a pictorial celebration of America / by the winners of
the Parade millennium photo contest ; introduction by Lee Kravitz.
p. cm.
ISBN 0-8264-1297-1
1. United States—Social life and customs—1971—Pictorial works.
I. Kravitz, Lee. II. Parade (New York, N.Y.)
E169.04 .F65 2000
973´.0022´2—dc21
00-043171

Poised for discovery.
Cassandra Coughlin, 4, is
totally focused on a
sudden visitor in the
butterfly house at New
York's Bronx Zoo. Photo
by her grandmother,
Sheryl Coughlin of
Saugus, Mass.

A new art movement—and it's about time. The artist, Hoop, hopes to move art
forward in the next century with his time-capsule truck. Self-portrait by
Stephen "Hoop" Hooper of Clifton, N.J.

Here, in this handsome and uplifting book, you'll encounter a vivid portrait of our nation and people as we enter the new millennium. It is America as seen through the eyes—and cameras—of the 100 winners of PARADE magazine's Millennium Photo Contest.

As Editor of PARADE, I've been impressed with the wide-ranging talents and interests of our readers. They number more than 80 million and represent, as well as anything I know, a true cross-section of this great country. They are thoughtful, curious and strong in their convictions. And, reflecting the best of America, they continually amaze me with their creativity and plain-spoken wisdom.

Still, I admit to having been surprised by the variety, scope and sheer humanity of the 120,000 photos submitted to our Millennium Photo Contest, nearly all taken by non-professionals. And I'm glad to report the same reaction from our distinguished judges—Eddie Adams, the Pulitzer Prize-winning photographer; Yogi Berra, the Hall of Fame catcher; Dr. Joyce Brothers, the psychologist and syndicated columnist; Enrico Colantoni, who plays a photographer on NBC's "Just Shoot Me!", and Marian Wright Edelman, the founder and president of the Children's Defense Fund and founder of Stand for Children Day.

There are dozens of fun, stirring and unforgettable images in this book—you'll find, for example, a cheerful motorist chauffeuring his two pet dogs; a little boy seeking to honor a forgotten soldier at the Vietnam Veterans Memorial; Comet Hale-Bopp streaking past a snow-covered evergreen. These photos capture the heart, soul and everyday realities of our nation as we journey into the twenty-first century. But they also remind us that, even as we pass from one millennium into another, certain values remain eternal—for all time.

So, welcome to our millennium picture gallery. We hope that you find it reflects your own hopes, dreams and lives.

—*Lee Kravitz*

Here comes the fun! The splendor of sunny days and summer vacation finally arrives for Alejandra Gonzalez. Photo by her father, Fred G. Gonzalez of San Diego, Calif.

A mermaid's tale (or tail?). The myth lives on in Samantha Rae Walker, 6 months, caught during bath time in the kitchen sink of her home in Bay Shore, N.Y. Photo by her grandmother, Lilliana of Bay Shore.

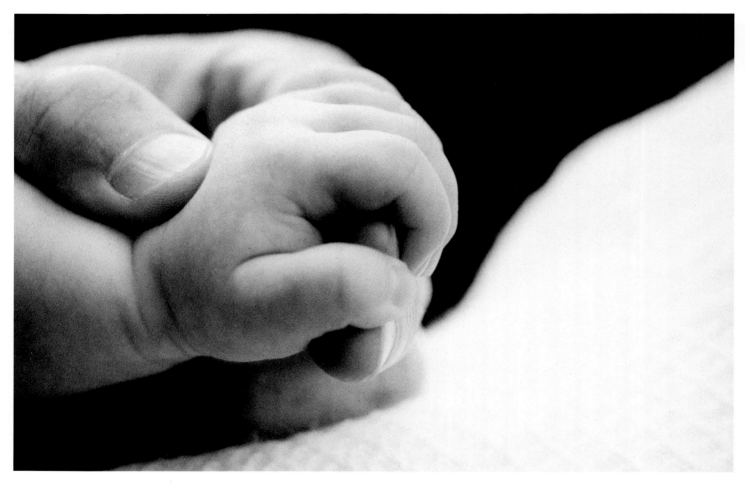

"You can hold on to me, son." Peter Kay, 37, of San Diego, Calif., shows Jonah, 2, a father's care. Jonah's mother, Jeni, chose a sepia color to preserve the warm moment.

Her first granddaughter. Neoma Adcox, 68, sees little Alise for the first time, in the arms of her proud papa, Michael Herring. Photo by Alise's aunt, Christi Adcox of Wilmington, N.C.

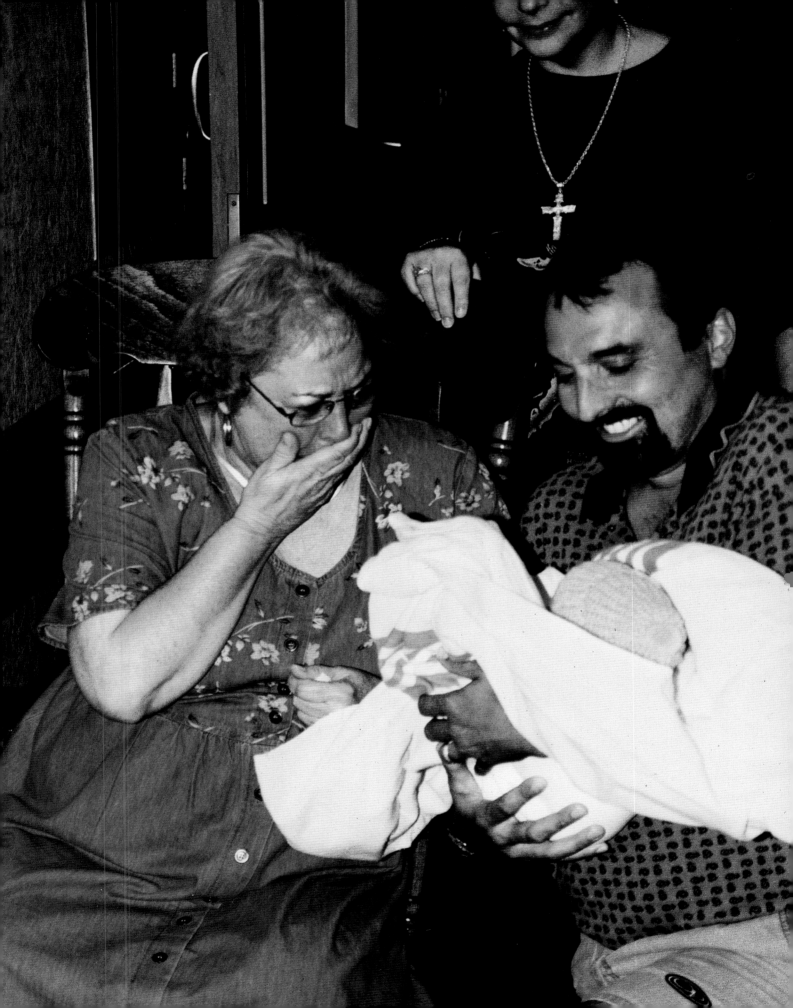

"Stick with me, kid."
Wiley Maddox, 5, shares
words of wisdom with
his brother Walt, 7
months, in their great-
grandparents' yard in
Bruce, Miss. Photo by
the boys' cousin, Holly
Mitchell, of Bruce.

"Welcome, little brother." Joseph Baycer, 3, meets Samuel, 5 days, for the first time. Photo by their mother, Margaret Baycer of Pittsburgh, Pa.

16

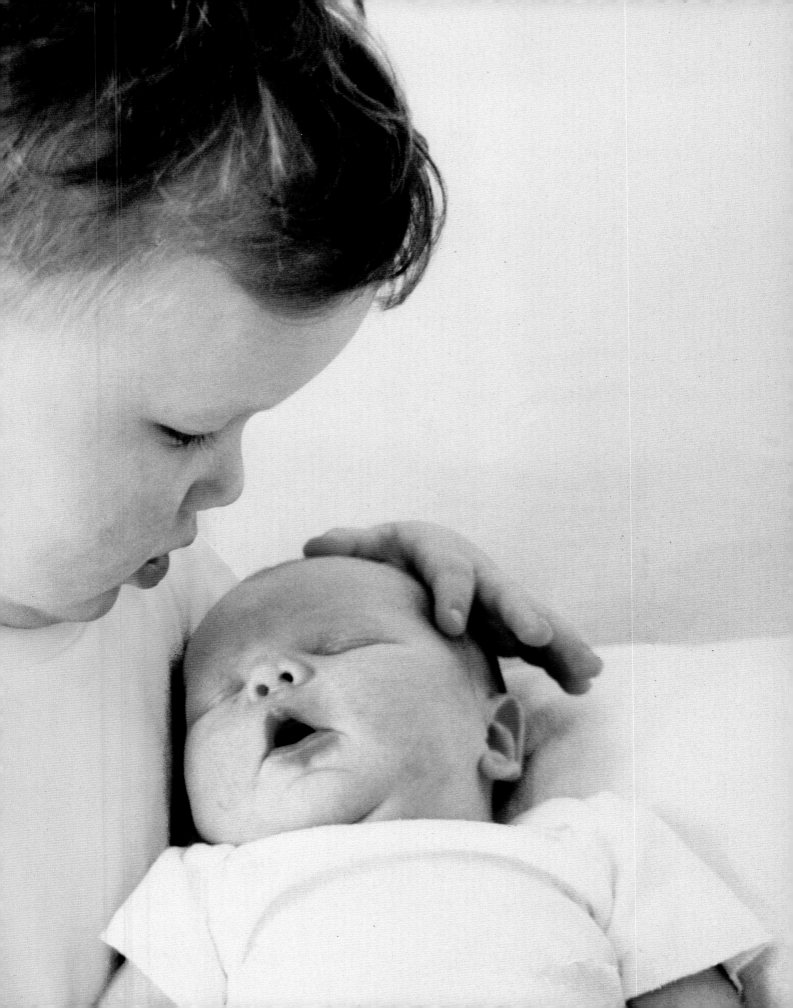

Blow me away! Mackenzie Steiner, 2, can't get enough of those magical bubbles during a visit with Aunt Wendy and Uncle John Robinson in Nashville, Tenn. Photo by her mom, Jamie Steiner of Virginia Beach, Va.

A moment to last a lifetime. Ronda Ruotolo, 20, of Troy, N.Y., enjoys her godchild, Jacob Toomey, 6 months. Photo by Ronda's mom, Alice Ruotolo Herald of Mechanicville, N.Y.

Like father, like son. Lance Jeffery Call, 3, clearly wants to grow up to be a firefighter just like his daddy, Douglas Lance Call, 37. Photo by Lance's mom, Beth Call of Fort Wayne, Ind.

Special delivery. Firefighter Thomas Lewandowski delivers his own son, Nicolas, in the hospital. The baby's mom, Kelly, said the picture was taken before Nicolas drew his first breath. Photo by Nicolas' grandmother, Trudy Fast of Toledo, Ohio.

He did it! Alexander Brant, 6, of Perryville, Md., goes for his first bike ride without the training wheels, followed by his proud dad, Andrew. "He has no idea Dad has let go, and he is on his own," says his mother, Beth Brant, who took the photo.

Walk this way. Cameron Coyne, 2, takes his ritual walk with his great-grandfather, John C. Allen, 88. Photo by Cameron's mother, Karen Coyne of Lompoc, Calif.

What a kiss! Diana
Vinsel Nemeth, 46,
puckers up for her
camera-shy son,
Joseph, 2, while her
husband, Hal, 39,
holds on. Photo taken in
the meditation garden
at Beacon House in
San Pedro, Calif.,
by Joseph's uncle,
Arthur R. Vinsel
of San Pedro.

A message for Grandma. C.J. Colletti, 3, hands a simple gift to his grandmother, Jan DiBella, in Wickham Park in Manchester, Conn. Photo by C.J.'s mom, Michele B. Colletti of Andover, Conn.

Golden slumber. Stone Smartt, 1 week old, rests in the arms of his father, Sean, who basks in the beauty of it all. Photo by Stone's mom, Pamela Smartt of North Highlands, Calif.

Spring's intoxicating
beauty. Joe Dudek of
Arlington, Tex.,
introduces his niece,
Kailey Ann Honolka, 19
months, to the season's
first azaleas. Photo by
Joe's wife, Susan, taken
in their backyard.

First smile. Tim Lander, 27, of Fort Worth, Tex., was the happiest dad in the world when Victoria, 9 weeks, smiled for a photo. Her mother, Roberta, captured the big moment.

"Oh, no! She's in the driver's seat already!" Alexandra Willard, 10, apparently feels quite at home behind the wheel—a shocking thought to her uncle, Frank Ashe. Photo by her dad, Randy Willard of Arlington, Va.

Watch out, Indiana Jones! Benjamin Goldberg (back row, center) enjoys his fifth birthday party with friends in his backyard. The party theme was "Safari Explorers." Photo by Benjamin's mother, Rayla Goldberg of Acworth, Ga.

Sharing the moment. Jake, 6, and Alexis Hiner, 9, of Acton,
Ind., enjoy the water fountain at a family picnic. Photo by
Steve Woerner of Indianapolis, Ind.

Wake us up for the millennium. Linda Vizzini of Fairview, Pa.,
placed Emily (l) and Maggie, her 2-month-old twin daughters,
on a blanket and began taking pictures. By the fourth shot,
she caught them agreeing that it was definitely naptime.

One special Sunday. Christina, 2, and Jennifer Scartelli, 4, of Bethlehem, Pa., in their matching Easter outfits. "Christina was crying, so Jennifer took her hand," says their mother, Susan Kent Scartelli, who took the photograph.

Open to experience. Benjamin Conroy (l) and Noah Sunflower, both 8, savor the first snowfall of winter 1992. Photo by Ben's mom, Nancy Johnston of Easton, Pa., who taught the boys in her home, a renovated one-room schoolhouse built in 1865. Ever the teacher, Nancy calls the event "Snowflake Eating 101."

Quiet time. Britain Hart (with bat), 7, and his brother, Hunter Pellichino, 4, take a break on a cool spring day in Hammond, La. Photo by Britain and Hunter's mom, Shelley Pellichino of Ponchatoula, La.

Now, listen up! Tim Miller, 35, gives the boys of the Owings Mills 9-10 A Travel baseball team (a.k.a. the Redbirds) one more pep talk before the big game. Alyssa Woods of Owings Mills, Md., shot this photo while her son, Matt (left, bottom), was too busy to notice.

With good friends, the party's never over. Jamie Filosa (l), 3,
and Olivia Groh can't stop celebrating Olivia's third birthday.
Photo by Sari A. Simon of Stamford, Conn.

Always ready to pose. Patrick Friday, 2, Priscilla Lowe, 3, and
Haley Treece, 3 (l-r), take a break from their morning search
for ducks to feed at Lake Elkhorn in Columbia, Md. Photo by
Priscilla's mom, Lisa Lowe of Columbia.

Barbershop solo. Christian Hoban, 2, hits a
note of protest over Tom Molettiere's
clippers. Photo taken at Molettiere's
Barber Shop in Lansdale, Pa., by Chris' mom,
Diane S. Hoban of Norristown, Pa.

Popsicle dreams. In a
rare moment of
stillness, the Weaver
brothers—Michael, 2,
and Geoffrey, 10—
savor one of life's
simple pleasures on
their front steps.
Photo by their mom,
Leslie Weaver of
Roanoke, Va.

So close, so fragile. Twin sisters Sarah (in glasses) and Hannah Franklin, 2, smooch in a patch of Texas bluebonnets near their house in Fort Worth, Tex. Five weeks later, Sarah died unexpectedly after surgery. "There were never any better friends than my sweet girls," says their mother, Stephanie, who took the photo.

A dancer's reverie. Kelsey Hanson, 3, seems to be choreographing a few steps of her own at a ballet class in Eugene, Ore. Photo by her dad, Mike Hanson of Creswell, Ore.

Here's looking at you, kid! Jensen McBean, 2, has a close encounter with a friendly dolphin at Sea World of Ohio. Photo by his mother, Kris McBean of Cement City, Mich.

A fair maiden rode out one day. Katelyn Gregory, 9, rides her pony, Missy, at her parents' farm in Edwardsburg, Mich. Photo by Bonnie Werntz of Mishawaka, Ind. (Katelyn usually wears a helmet, Bonnie says, but was allowed to remove it for the photo.)

Silent beauty. Claudia Murray plants zinnias in her backyard in Jamestown, N.C., because she loves watching—and photographing—the butterflies that visit to gather nectar. "There is a silent beauty in nature," she says, "and many beautiful messages, if we just take the time to observe and listen."

All in a day's work. A camel takes a breather from carrying tourists at the pyramids in Giza, Egypt. Photo by Brian Zemba of League City, Tex.

What's your hurry? The ducks on South Main Street in Allentown, N.J., help their neighbors to slow down. Besides...they're going places too! Photo by Michael Tozzi of Hamilton, N.J.

The best things in life. James Andrew Lindler with his dog, Jake, tends his corn and potatoes in the early morning sun. "His garden was his pride and joy," says his son, James Richard Lindler of Chapin, S.C., who took the photo in 1988. James Sr. died three years later at age 85.

Concerned parents. Early one morning, Brother John E. Argauer of Maryknoll Fathers and Brothers came upon this swan family in the shallows of Twin Lakes in Tarrytown, N.Y.

Cat's cradle. Pauline Elizabeth Willis Godard holds a precious gift on her 99th birthday. Photo by her daughter, Alice Godard Weber of Jonesboro, Ga.

The joy of the ride is "the girls" by your side. The open road awaits Rocky Ferrell and sisters, Aussie (l) and Bud. Photo by his wife, Gloria Montejo Ferrell of Tucson, Ariz.

The way we were.
Robert Shelburne
Ruddick Jr., 79, and his
wife, Louise, 75,
celebrate their 50th
wedding anniversary.
Photo by their
daughter, Beth Ruddick
Sinnenberg of
Richmond, Va.

The life we've shared. Arlene and Robert Chestnut, retired farmers, now watch the world together. Photo by their daughter, Carol Konkol of Charlotte, N.C.

"Will you be mine?" The only thing left was to give her
the ring. For the occasion, Richard Brower, 23, took
his fiancée, Wendy George, 21, to Provo Canyon, Utah.
Wendy's mom, Joan George of Irvine, Calif., went
along to catch the moment.

"I only have eyes for you." On a sunrise bike tour in Maui, Janet and Jim Witherspoon greet the dawn—their way—at the top of the Haleakala volcano in Hawaii. Photo by Norma Evans of West Valley City, Utah.

66

"My mommy's the best...*Boo-hoo!*" Tina Haag's success—commencement speaker at her graduation in March 1999 with a degree in business from the University of Phoenix—was too much to bear for her daughter, Cassandra, 4, but not for her son, Austin, 6. Photo by Tina's proud mother, Sandra Maeser of Tucson, Ariz.

Bubbles of bliss. Dr. and Mrs. Clint Holumzer are simply buoyant on their wedding day. Photo by Annamaria Nagy of Phoenix, Ariz.

"Aren't I a little too old for this?" Eric Klooster, 23,
is congratulated by his proud parents, Alex and Beverly
Klooster, at his commencement ceremony at Calvin College
in Grand Rapids, Mich. Photo by Eric's wife, Andrea Klooster
of Grandville, Mich.

"I made it!" Attica Georges, 26, beams with pride after receiving two undergraduate degrees—one in accounting, the other in finance—from the School of Business at California State University. Photo by Attica's aunt, Arabella Grayson of Emeryville, Calif.

A century of living. Margaret King—great-great-grandmother of 11—prepares to blow out the candles on her 100th birthday. Photo by her granddaughter, Shirley Mendonca of North Dartmouth, Mass.

A sweet 91 party. Virginia Pope Evans of Carmel, Calif., celebrates her birthday with bubbly—and turns her age on its head! Photo by Katy Stock of Monterey, Calif.

On fire. The national tae kwon do title was at stake with one match to go. The South Region girls team (10- to 12-year-old black belts) was a person short, so someone would have to fight a second time—against the reigning division champion. Cassandra Mazur, 12, took the challenge, won a tough match and victory for her team. Photo, taken immediately after the match, by Sandra Howard Mazur of Plano, Tex.

All for one, and one for all! St. Didacus School cheerleaders Angela Watkins, Brittany Bodie and Whitney Mayoras (l-r), all 13, head home after a football game. Photo by Whitney's mom, Tina Mayoras of San Diego, Calif.

Youthful serenity.
Two boys peer
out from a
monastery in Laos.
Photo by Peter
Whittlesey of
Oroville, Calif.

Ride 'em, cowboy! Nathaniel Wyman, 16, of Apple Valley, Calif.,
celebrates his hike up to Wild Bull Rock at Zion National Park
in Utah. Photo by Jeffrey Taylor of Apple Valley.

Nature's sudden beauty. David Lincicome of Issaquah, Wash.,
caught a rainbow in the spray from the geyser Old Faithful
at Yellowstone Park, Wyo.

Electric city. Nature strikes the night sky of downtown Chicago, captured by Alberto E. Rodriguez, a resident of the Windy City.

Timeless tombs. The great pyramids in Giza, Egypt—built to provide deceased royalty with a suitable resting place before entering the next life—have stood for more than 4000 years. Photo by James R. Holland of Boston, Mass.

Puddle of love. It was Valentine's Day, the rain had stopped, and suddenly there it was— in the driveway of Carol Welk's home in Columbia, Md. So she grabbed her camera.

Down a shady lane. In a tree-lined arcade on the grounds of the Het Loo, a summer residence for Dutch royalty, two unknown children make their way through the light and shadow. Photo taken in Apeldoorn, Netherlands, by Julie Sprott of Anchorage, Alaska.

Serenity. David Wolf enjoys a quiet moment on a bridge spanning the Charles River in Boston. Photo by his wife, Jamie Wolf of Beverly Hills, Calif.

Bucolic blessings. Like early Americans, folks in rural communities continue to attend small churches in the wilderness. This one is in the Great Smoky Mountains in Cades Cove, Tenn. Photo by William L. Deaton of Morgantown, W.Va.

Growing together. Six redwoods reach for the sky near the Scotts Valley cabin of the Wiele family of Escalon, Calif. Photo by Brian Wiele.

Eternal cycles. An ancient Jeffrey pine tree endures as the sun sets and a full moon rises in California's Yosemite National Park. Photo by Steve Harding of Mariposa, Calif.

What others risk for us. As part of a program to educate residents, firefighters in Tallahassee, Fla., created a citizens' academy to teach them the techniques of fighting a blaze firsthand (using a propane gas fire). Photo was taken at the Firefighting Training Center by Kay Arnold Caster of Tallahassee.

Leave your watch at home. Tom Belzowski of LaPorte, Ind., took this photo of his son, Keith, 18, one evening while fishing together on nearby Pine Lake.

Independence Day. Michael Sycz, 7, of North Ridgeville, Ohio, celebrates the holiday at the Erie, Pa., home of his grandmother, Patricia "Nana" Matczak, overlooking Lake Erie. Photo by Nana.

Patriot's gate. While passing through Ouray, Colo., on vacation, Randy and Judy Sorenson of Salt Lake City, Utah, spotted this striking front yard. Randy took the photo from their car.

Celebrating America— and us! Naomi and "Gino" Genarie spend a Memorial Day at Leisure World of Maryland in Silver Spring. Photo by Marion L. Polli of Silver Spring, Md.

Floating on Stars and Stripes. Patriotism is unflagging in the
annual "Yankee Homecoming" Parade in Newburyport, Mass.
Photo by Alan Bazer of Newburyport.

Reflection and remembrance. Paul Gottlieb, 36, touches the etched names on the Korean War Memorial in Washington, D.C. Photo by his wife, Leah Gottlieb of Franklin, Va.

USSELL L PRICE ·

Veterans Memorial

A FERR

LLS · BC

EUSTAC

RD D AL

PAUL M

PETERS

ARTLET

He won't forget. A boy etches a name from the Vietnam Veterans War Memorial in Washington, D.C. Celia Deaton, a photography student from Morgantown, W.Va., took the picture on a visit with her father, a Vietnam War veteran.

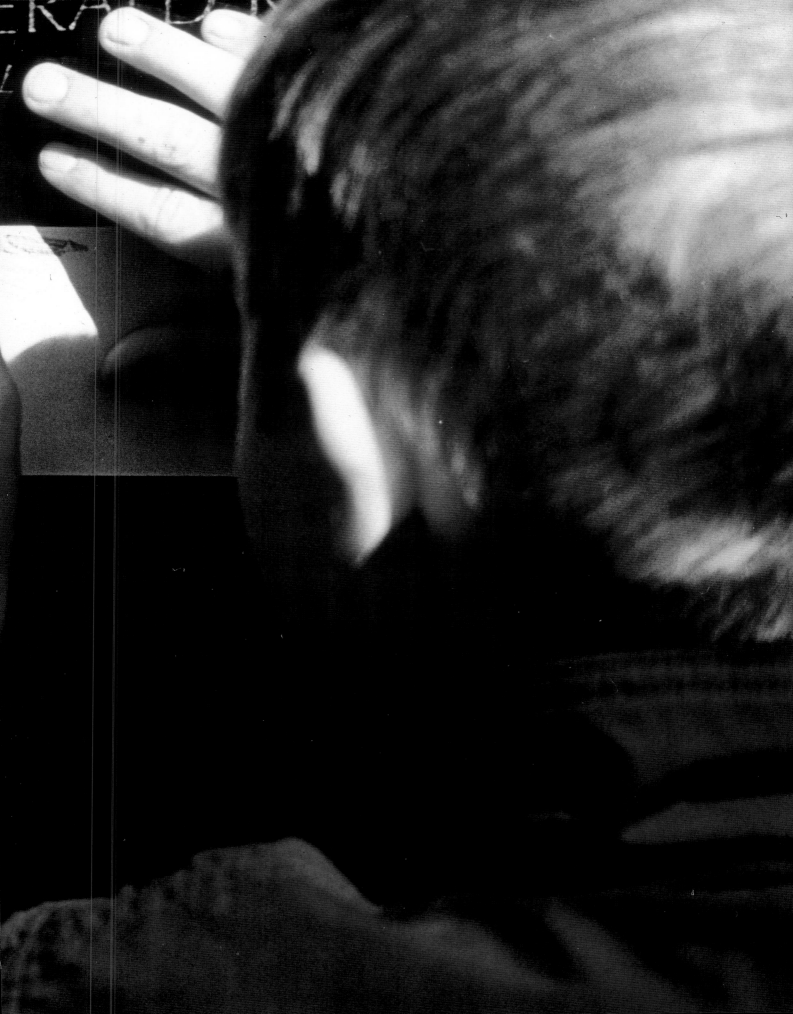

At journey's end. Katherine Howell says
farewell to her husband, James Howell—a
Marine who served in WWII—at Riverside
Memorial Park in Jacksonville, Fla.
Photo by her daughter-in-law, Joan Howell
of Jacksonville.

First salute. Chance
Chambers (r), 4, and
Cooper Early, 3, join
their grandfather, Allen
Lewison, on the banks of
the Withlacooche River
in Dunellon, Fla., to
honor those who served
on Memorial Day, 1999.
Photo by Cooper's mom,
Stacey Early of
Clearwater, Fla.

My inspiration. Alan Blume, 40, who has cerebral palsy, serves on the Transit Authority's handicapped advisory committee in Washington, D.C. Mary Louise Wilen of Springfield, Va. took this photo at the FDR Memorial in Washington. Alan visits the memorial to his favorite President often, says Mary.

LOW COUNTRYMEN · AT THIS SECOND
·RING TO TAKE THE OATH OF THE PRES-
TIAL OFFICE THERE IS LESS OCCASION
AN EXTENDED ADDRESS THAN THERE
AT THE FIRST · THEN A STATEMENT
WHAT IN DETAIL OF A COURSE TO BE
JED SEEMED FITTING AND PROPER ·
AT THE EXPIRATION OF FOUR YEARS
NG WHICH PUBLIC DECLARATIONS
BEEN CONSTANTLY CALLED FORTH
VERY POINT AND PHASE OF THE GREAT
ST WHICH STILL ABSORBS THE AT-
ON AND ENGROSSES THE ENERGIES
HE NATION LITTLE THAT IS NEW
BE PRESENTED · THE PROGRESS OF
RMS UPON WHICH ALL ELSE CHIEFLY
DS IS AS WELL KNOWN TO THE PUBLIC
MYSELF AND IT IS I TRUST REASON-
ATISFACTORY AND ENCOURAGING TO
ITH HIGH HOPE FOR THE FUTURE NO
TION IN REGARD TO IT IS VENTURED ·
THE OCCASION CORRESPONDING TO
UR YEARS AGO ALL THOUGHTS WERE
USLY DIRECTED TO AN IMPENDING
VAR · ALL DREADED IT · ALL SOUGHT
RT IT · WHILE THE INAUGURAL AD-
WAS BEING DELIVERED FROM THIS
DEVOTED ALTOGETHER TO SAVING
NION WITHOUT WAR INSURGENT
WERE IN THE CITY SEEKING TO DE-
T WITHOUT WAR · SEEKING TO DIS-
HE UNION AND DIVIDE EFFECTS BY
ATION · BOTH PARTIES DEPRECATED
T ONE OF THEM WOULD MAKE WAR
THAN LET THE NATION SURVIVE

AND THE OTHER WOULD ACCEPT WAR RATHER
THAN LET IT PERISH · AND THE WAR CAME
ONE EIGHTH OF THE WHOLE POPULATION WERE
COLORED SLAVES NOT DISTRIBUTED GENERAL-
LY OVER THE UNION BUT LOCALIZED IN THE
SOUTHERN PART OF IT · THESE SLAVES CONSTI-
TUTED A PECULIAR AND POWERFUL INTEREST ·
ALL KNEW THAT THIS INTEREST WAS SOMEHOW
THE CAUSE OF THE WAR · TO STRENGTHEN PER-
PETUATE AND EXTEND THIS INTEREST WAS THE
OBJECT FOR WHICH THE INSURGENTS WOULD
REND THE UNION EVEN BY WAR WHILE THE GOV-
ERNMENT CLAIMED NO RIGHT TO DO MORE
THAN TO RESTRICT THE TERRITORIAL ENLARGE-
MENT OF IT · NEITHER PARTY EXPECTED FOR
THE WAR THE MAGNITUDE OR THE DURATION
WHICH IT HAS ALREADY ATTAINED · NEITHER
ANTICIPATED THAT THE CAUSE OF THE CONFLICT
MIGHT CEASE WITH OR EVEN BEFORE THE CON-
FLICT ITSELF SHOULD CEASE · EACH LOOKED FOR
AN EASIER TRIUMPH AND A RESULT LESS FUN-
DAMENTAL AND ASTOUNDING · BOTH READ THE
SAME BIBLE AND PRAY TO THE SAME GOD AND
EACH INVOKES HIS AID AGAINST THE OTHER ·
IT MAY SEEM STRANGE THAT ANY MEN SHOULD
DARE TO ASK A JUST GOD'S ASSISTANCE IN
WRINGING THEIR BREAD FROM THE SWEAT OF
OTHER MEN'S FACES · BUT LET US JUDGE NOT
THAT WE BE NOT JUDGED · THE PRAYERS OF BOTH
COULD NOT BE ANSWERED · THAT OF NEITHER
HAS BEEN ANSWERED FULLY · THE ALMIGHTY
HAS HIS OWN PURPOSES · "WOE UNTO THE WORLD
BECAUSE OF OFFENSES FOR IT MUST NEEDS BE
THAT OFFENSES COME BUT WOE TO THAT MAN
BY WHOM THE OFFENSE COMETH ·"

Summer's end. Caroline Meehan, 8, snuggles up to her great aunt
Vera, 74, at the family's vacation home in Atlantic Beach, N.C.
Photo by Caroline's mom, Susan Meehan of Paoli, Pa.

Those words still loom
large. Tony Mancuso
visits the Lincoln
Memorial in Washington,
D.C., on his seventh
birthday. The trip to the
nation's capital was a
gift from his parents.
Photo by Tony's dad,
Roger Mancuso of
Newfoundland, Pa.

"See, kid, it's really easy."
O. Leon Silbermann, 81,
teaches his youngest
grandson, Matt, 3, to
ride his tricycle. Photo
by Matt's mom, Janet
Burgermeister of
Bethlehem, Pa.

An early start. Adam Duke Smith, 9 months, follows along as his grandfather, Darryl J. Lambertson, 54, reads him a story. Photo by Adam's grandmother, Carla Lambertson of Oxford, Mich.

If this moment could last forever. It was a happy day for
Mildred Sherburne, 87, when her nieces—Ellen Merick (r) of
North Pole, Alaska, and Milly Goode of Canby, Ore.—traveled
to Clarksville, Iowa, to pay her a special visit. Goode's photo
captured the warmth they all felt.

Unconditional love. Dollie Scruggs, 79, hugs
her great-great-niece, Angel Childress, 1,
on their front porch. Dollie and her husband,
James, are raising the toddler. Photo by
Allison Lewis of Huntsville, Ala.

Generation sandwich.
Kaylie Saidin, 8 months,
poses with her dad, Zain
Saidin, 30, and granddad,
Ahmad Saidin, 58, during
some treasured "family
time." Photo by Diana
Saidin of Sunnyvale, Calif.

Across the generations. Ellie Mae Wasserman, 3, and her great-grandmother, Esther Chalif, 78, can't seem to get enough of one another. Photo by Ellie Mae's grandmother, Linda Wasserman of La Jolla, Calif.

"Grandpa, I'll help you!"
Kaitlin Searfoss, 5,
eagerly runs to assist
her grandfather,
Harutun Kehian, 80,
who was recovering
from hip surgery. Photo
by Louise Maciejewski
of Walpole, Mass.

Happy birthday, Great-Granddad. Fred Petrick welcomes a surprise from his great-granddaughters, Amanda Carson, 9, and Whitney Carson, 10, at his 90th birthday celebration. Photo by Lisa Carson of Swisher, Iowa.

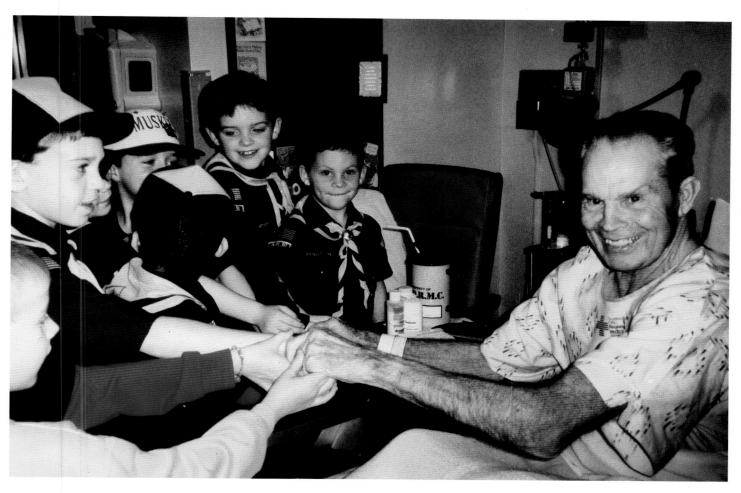

Good deed. Members of Cub Scout Pack 510 in New Concord, Ohio, cheer up Homer Chambers on a visit to the Southeastern Ohio Regional Medical Center in nearby Cambridge. Photo by Melanie Jeskey of Norwich, Ohio.

"We'll sit this one out." Jean Kinney of Silver Spring, Md., was snapping pictures at Atlantic Beach, N.C., when she came upon these sunbathers. "I just knew I had to take it," she says.

I remember them well. The hands are those of Margaret Clark, at 94. The portrait she's holding, taken in 1927, shows her young son, James N. Clark— father-to-be of Brad Clark of Lincoln, Neb., who took this photo in 1994. Margaret and James are both gone now, though not in Brad's heart.

Old friends. Margaret Marsh, 87, who lives at St. Anne's Hospice, and John "Barney" Barnholtz, 84, who lives at Watkins Home, both in Winona, Minn., meet daily to feed the ducks at Lake Winona and enjoy each other's company. Photo by Andy Ducett of Winona.

A tradition lives on. Every Christmas, Richard L. Sizemore, 38, and his family would visit his 87-year-old grandmother, Gladys R. McPeak, to sing carols. Although she's now in a nursing home, the family continues its holiday visits. Photo by Michelle Dix of Wytheville, Va.

Hello again. This photo of Comet Hale-Bopp—last seen from Earth around 2200 B.C.—was shot March 26, 1997, along U.S. Highway 50 by Paul Nelson of Grand Junction, Colo. He used a 35-second exposure and strobe lights to illuminate the evergreen tree, anonymously decorated by passersby.

Modern focus, ancient ways. A hardworking
video technician captures the traditional
festivities on tape at The Confederated
Tribes of Grand Ronde Annual Pow-Wow in
Grand Ronde, Ore. Elizabeth McClure of
Salem, Ore., captured him on film.

Think global, shoot
local. Beccah Maskin, 17,
a student in Delmar,
N.Y., used a large
reflecting ball to
reimagine her home and
garden—and herself.

Together, we are mighty. To promote dependence on one another as a team, the coach of this Seattle soccer squad had the players perform the exercise of linking arms and wading as far as possible into the ocean surf without breaking the link. Photo by James M. Keough of Edmonds, Wash.

Terminated? Never! Sandra Jo Williams of
Amarillo, Tex., took this shot of a house
destroyed by a tornado in Moore, Okla.

...And a time to reap.
LaVerne Mikkelson, 53,
checks the progress of
his durum wheat field
near Minot, N.D. Photo
by his wife, Kandi.

They're all set. Amy (l), 3, and Abby Welton,
2, of Baker, Fla., share a giggle as they get
a new "do" from their mom, Molly Welton,
who also took the photo.

Peak performance.
Sisters Marjorie Carol
Frank Northern, 59, and
R. Rosalyn Frank Clark,
62, reach the summit of
Clifty Mountain in
Idaho. Photo by Bob
Clark of Sagle, Idaho.

EDDIE ADAMS

As you look through this winning collection of photographs, I want you to take your time. I know it seems impossible to escape from the inexorable drone of the minutes flying by, reminding you of everything you should be busy doing, everywhere you need to be.

But at its most sublime, a photograph overthrows the dictates of time and space and invites you into this unearthly dimension where one sweet slice of a second suddenly crystallizes into an eternity.

The moments captured in these photographs beg to be saved and savored—the volcanic elation of a kiss at dawn, the beatific vision of a newborn asleep against his father's skin, the ethereal aura of Comet Hale-Bopp streaming past an ancient evergreen.

I was particularly struck by how these photos squeeze out the quintessence of human experience—from the milestones to the mundane. Can't you just taste the chill of a creamsicle on a summer day? Hear the shriek of a two year old beneath the barber's clippers? Feel the breathless gasp of a grandmother as she sees her very first grandchild?

Choosing only 100 photographs "for all time" was a formidable task. So I tried to keep my criteria as simple as possible. Without the aid of a caption or explanation, with nothing more than the image in my palm—it had to win my heart. And I predict that our selections will continue to win hearts for generations to come. All of these photographs remind me of why I fell in love with my camera so many years ago, and why I fall in love with America all over again each and every day.

People say I'm famous for saying, "The future ain't what it used to be." But as I looked at this year's winners, I can say that despite all the technological advances in the last century, many things like love, loyalty, humor and adventure never change.

I've had a lot of fun being a judge for PARADE's Millennium Photo Contest. I've seen winners, losers and many heroes over the years, so being asked to pick the very best images of the millennium was a great challenge. History books will attempt to explain this century, but there is something only a photograph can do. How can you sum up a whole century in one image? It's tough.

I looked for the pictures that captured those things that sustain us and bring us together. The qualities of life that show love and courage, like the determination of a Seattle soccer squad learning to depend on each other by linking arms and plunging into the icy ocean, or the wonder of a little girl looking into the wise eyes of her great-grandmother.

I particularly liked the funny ones, like Rocky Ferrell in his pickup truck beside his two loyal dogs, or the two boys catching the first snowfall of the year on their tongues. There was Alejandra Gonzalez leaping for joy through her backyard sprinkler and the timeless photo of a North Dakota farmer out checking his wheat field.

I went from playing ball with a broom and a bottle cap as a boy in St. Louis to 14 World Series and the Baseball Hall of Fame this century. A lot has happened in my lifetime, but some things...well, they probably won't ever change. Congratulations to all the winners. Job well done. Like I've always said, "You can observe a lot just by watchin'."

And what about the next century? Well...it ain't over till it's over.

YOGI BERRA

Resilience and resolve are two singular qualities of the human spirit that continually enthrall me—even after more than 30 years of helping people overcome adversity. While judging this year's contest, I realized that these qualities echo the theme "For All Time." In a world measured in nanoseconds, replete with change, few elements endure but that of the human will.

From a week-old newborn to a centenarian, the individuals depicted in these photographs are an amalgam of the contradictions and continuities that delineate Americans today. Yet the occasions rendered on these pages—travels, births, cultural celebrations—reflect the past as much as they portend the future. Our nation's ability to reinvent itself in order to flourish resides in the faces we see here.

In this montage are myriad examples of what it means to strive toward an ideal. Eclectic but classic, these snapshots elicit nostalgia, admiration—even mirth. The composition varies, but the message behind them clearly is for all time.

DR. JOYCE BROTHERS

ENRICO COLANTONI

"**P**oint, click and shoot" boasts a recent ad slogan for a new, easy-to-use camera. I have discovered through my role in television, and by looking at the photographs in the contest, the emotion that goes into the process of taking pictures. Actually, a photograph is more than a picture—it's a story.

The amateur shutterbugs who took these photos have a personal connection to their subject matter that a professional often does not. Whether it be a thread from the tapestry of family, nature, history or society, each moment on film is borrowed from that person's life. These images encompass a broad landscape of our world today—scenes from the cosmic to the subterranean—proving that the personal is indeed universal. The interpretations of the contest motif constructed by our winners abound in creative introspection. Sentiments that allude to such time-tested virtues as teamwork, scholarship and honor are represented. All of the PARADE readers who entered their photographs not only entertained but also shared with us a part of their individuality.

These photographs show the wide spectrum of families across America and the places and people that make us happy. They display the qualities we like best about ourselves: our thoughtfulness, humor, grace, kindness.

Many of these faces are the emblems of my dreams for our time. The photographs capture, at least for a moment, the best part of us. It is my dream that every person experience a rich and color-drenched childhood. I want every child to know what it feels like to spread their arms open wide, lift their eyes to the sky and feel the sunlight warm their bodies and smell azaleas in full bloom. It is my dream that every person have a strong and vital family, and know what it means to be held, nurtured and protected. I see in the little girl laughing in the arms of her adoring great-great aunt such a fine future. It is my dream that every child have someone who believes in her. If only there were a hand holding onto the back of every first bicycle until it's time to let go so that all of our children might sail safely into adulthood.

So much life, so many extraordinary memories are preserved in this collection. Now we must save the lives on our streets, in our homes and on the margins. The next generation will know not only the people we choose to immortalize but also the people we leave behind. I hope these pictures inspire you to share my dreams for America's families and help to make them reality.

MARIAN WRIGHT EDELMAN